Weekly Reader Books presents

HELP IS ON
THE WAY
FOR:

Thinking
Skills

Written by Marilyn Berry
Pictures by Bartholomew

Living Skills Productions
Fallbrook, California

Producer: Marilyn Berry
Editor: Theresa Tinkle
Consultants: Jim Reith and Terie Snyder
Design and Art Direction: Abigail Johnston
Typesetting: Curt Chelin

For a complete catalog of other living skills materials,
write to: Institute of Living Skills
P.O. Box 1461, Fallbrook, CA 92028

So you need to work on your **thinking skills!**

Hang on! Help is on the way!

If you are having a hard time
- making decisions,
- solving problems, or
- knowing if something is true or untrue...

...you are not alone!

Just in case you're wondering. . .

. . .why don't we start at the beginning?

What Are Thinking Skills?

Thinking is a mental activity that can take on many forms. When you think, you may be
- forming an opinion or belief,
- remembering,
- reasoning,
- creating ideas, or
- learning.

A *skill* is an ability that comes with training and practice. A *thinking skill* is the ability to help your mind do its job with more success and less frustration. Thinking skills help you to get your mind organized.

There are three major types of thinking skills:
- Decision-making skills
- Problem-solving skills
- Critical thinking skills

If you will learn and practice these skills, your mind will work more efficiently, and your life will run more smoothly.

Your mind is a storehouse for a wealth of information. Your mind also continues to take in new information every day. Thinking skills will help you to get the most out of this information. Learning thinking skills can be easy if you take it one step at a time.

Decision-Making Skills

To decide means to make a choice between two or more alternatives. When you are in a situation that calls for a decision, decision-making skills will help you choose the *best* alternative.

You may not realize it, but you make many decisions every day. For example, you decide
- what to wear,
- whom you want to be with,
- where you want to go, and
- what you want to do.

These decisions are usually easy to make. However, there will be times when you need to make more difficult decisions.

There are six simple steps to making a good decision:
1. State the question.
2. List your goals.
3. List your alternatives.
4. Gather some information.
5. Consider and compare your alternatives.
6. Make your decision.

Step One: State The Question

The first step in decision-making is to determine exactly *what* you need to decide. It is best to make just one decision at a time. Most often it will be in the form of a question.

Try to keep the question simple.
State the question clearly and write it down.

Step Two: List Your Goals

Once you have stated the question, the next step is to list your goals. Your goals should include the things you hope to accomplish by making your decision. Write down your goals in the order of importance. Put the most important goals at the top of the list and the least important goals at the bottom.

Step Three: List Your Alternatives

Your next step is to make a list of the alternatives open to you. Try not to settle for only the obvious alternatives. Try to add different and creative alternatives to your list. You might want to discuss your situation with another person to see if he or she can suggest alternatives you have not thought of.

Step Four: Gather Some Information

In order to make an intelligent decision, you need to gather some information about each of your alternatives. You will want to look for the good and bad points of each possible choice. Be sure to include *any* information that could help you with your final decision.

An important part of gathering information is to consider the consequences or outcome of each alternative.

- Consider your first alternative. Try to imagine what would happen if you chose that alternative.
- Try to decide whether or not the consequences would be good or bad.
- Do this with each alternative.

Make Alternative Charts. It will be easier to gather information and to make your final decision if you make some simple charts.

- List each alternative on a separate piece of paper.
- Under each alternative draw two columns and label them ''Pro'' (which means *for*) and ''Con'' (which means *against*).
- Under the ''Pro'' column, list all the information that makes the alternative a good choice.
- Under the ''Con'' column, list all the information that makes the alternative a bad choice.

The Life of Louis Pasteur

PRO	CON
1. Lots of information available	1. Could not enter in Science Fair
2. Fits the assignment	2. Not an unusual project
3. Fairly easy project	3. Not very interesting to me

Step Five: Consider And Compare Your Alternatives

Once you have gathered all the information you need, it's time to consider and compare your alternatives.

- Get out your list of goals.
- Get out your alternative charts.
- Compare each alternative with your list of goals.
- Look closely at the "Pros" and "Cons" of each alternative.
- Look at the consequences of each alternative.

Step Six: Make Your Decision

If you have carefully followed the first five steps, most of the time the best alternative will surface and your decision will be made for you. When that does not happen, you will need to make a choice between your best alternatives. Since decisions don't *always* work out as planned, it is wise to have a "backup" alternative.

Follow-Up

You can learn from the decision you made if you will take the time to determine whether or not your decision was a good one. Ask yourself these questions:

- ''Were the results what I expected?''
- ''What went right?''
- ''What went wrong?''
- ''Did I gather enough information?''
- ''What would I do differently?''

Problem-Solving Skills

A *problem* is a difficult situation that needs to be worked out. *To solve* means to find an answer to a difficult situation. When you find yourself in a difficult situation, problem-solving skills will help you find a solution.

Everybody has problems. You will occasionally
have problems, too. Some of your problems will
be more difficult to solve than others. No matter
how difficult your problem, solving it will be
easier if you follow the problem-solving steps.

There are five easy steps to solving a problem:
1. State the problem.
2. List the possible solutions.
3. Gather some information.
4. Consider and compare the solutions.
5. Choose a solution.

Step One: State The Problem

The first step in problem-solving is to determine exactly what the problem is. It is best to solve just one problem at a time. There are two rules to follow.

1. Don't confuse the problem with unimportant points.

2. Try to keep the problem simple and to the point. State the problem clearly and write it down.

Step Two: List The Possible Solutions

Your next step is to make a list of all the possible solutions to your problem. Try not to limit yourself to only the obvious solutions. Try to add different and creative solutions to your list.

Step Three: Gather Some Information

The next step toward solving your problem is to gather some information about each of the possible solutions. You will be looking for both the good and bad points of each solution. Be sure to include *any* information that could help you come to your final conclusion.

An important part of gathering information is to consider the consequences or outcome of each solution.

- Consider your first solution. Try to imagine what would happen if you chose that solution.
- Try to decide whether or not the consequences would be good or bad.
- Do this with each solution.

Make a Solution Chart. It will be easier to gather and organize your information if you make a solution chart. You will need a large piece of paper and a pencil.

To make the chart:
- Draw a column for each possible solution on your list.
- Label each column with a solution.
- Divide each column in half.
- Label one side of each column "Pro" and the other side "Con."

To use the chart:
- Go over the information you gathered about your first solution.
- On the "Pro" side of the column, write down all the information that makes it a good solution.
- On the "Con" side of the column, write down all the information that makes it a bad solution.
- Do this for each possible solution.

Solution #1 Choose up sides Mixing Boys With Girls		Solution #2 Alternate turns each recess		Solution #3 Girls against Boys		Solution #4 First come, first served	
PRO	CON	PRO	CON	PRO	CON	PRO	CON
1. Both groups get to play	1. Takes too much time						
2. You can choose own teams	2. Boys don't want to play with girls						
3. It may help boys and girls get along better	3. Girls don't want to play with boys						
	4. There are too many people for two teams						

Step Four: Consider And Compare The Solutions

Once you have gathered all the information you need, it's time to think about the possible solutions.

- Look carefully at the "Pros" and "Cons" of each solution.
- Eliminate the solutions that have more important "Cons" than "Pros."
- Choose the best solution from the ones remaining.

Step Five: Choose A Situation

If you have carefully followed the first four steps, you have probably found a good solution. But remember, solutions should be flexible. You may want to revise your solution to make it fit your exact situation.

Test Your Solution. Before you settle completely on the solution you have chosen, you may want to give it a *trial period* to see how well it works.

- Decide on a fair amount of time to allow the solution to work. This will be your trial period.
- Try the solution.
- At the end of the trial period, evaluate how well the solution is working.
- Adjust the solution or try a new solution if necessary.

Critical Thinking Skills

To *think critically* means to evaluate carefully what another person says or writes.

Critical thinking skills help you to decide if what another person says or writes is true or not true.

Every day you are presented with new information. It is up to you to decide whether or not the information is accurate and true. This task will be easier if you learn to
- listen with a critical ear and
- read with a critical eye.

The key to critical thinking is learning how to ask the right questions.

There are three major steps to thinking critically:
1. Find out if the speaker is reliable.
2. Make sure you understand the information.
3. Look for tricks meant to persuade you.

Step One: Find Out If The Speaker Is Reliable

Your first step is to find out if you can trust the speaker. Ask yourself these questions:
- "Is the speaker qualified to speak on the subject?"
- "Is the speaker giving facts or just opinion?"
- "Does the speaker present both sides of the story?"
- "What do other experts say on the same subject?"

You will also want to question the speaker's sources. Ask yourself these questions:
- "Where did the speaker get the information?"
- "Is the information current?"
- "Are there new or additional facts that I need to consider?"

Step Two:
Make Sure You Understand The Information

If you don't understand what a person is saying, you can't decide whether or not the information is true. You can solve this problem by asking these questions:

- "Do I understand all the words the speaker is using?" If not, look up any words you don't know or ask the speaker to explain them.

- "Do I understand all of the points that the speaker is trying to present?" It may help to write down each point as it is presented. Don't forget to look for points that are suggested but not actually stated.

Step Three:
Look For Tricks Meant To Persuade You

There are many tricks that a speaker can use to talk you into believing something that is not true. Beware! And ask yourself these questions:

- "Is the speaker trying to play on my emotions?" Some speakers try to convince you of something by making you feel a certain way, such as guilty or sorry.

- "Is the speaker using loaded words to persuade me?" *Loaded words* are used by people to change or distort the facts to make you feel a certain way. *Neutral words* present only the facts. For example:

  The man put the **brown** dog in the truck.
  The man put the **vicious** dog in the truck.
  The man put the **frail** dog in the truck.

The first sentence uses neutral words. The last two sentences use loaded words.

- "Does the speaker make clear what is fact and what is opinion?" Some speakers try to disguise their opinions by stating them as facts.

You won't master these thinking skills overnight.
It takes practice. But every time you
• make a decision,
• solve a problem, or
• decide whether or not something is true,
you will become better at your thinking skills.

WARNING!

If you try the ideas in this book, your life will probably run more smoothly and...

...your mind will love you for it!

THE END

About the Author
Marilyn Berry has a master's degree in education with a specialization in reading. She is on staff as a creator of supplementary materials at Living Skills Press. Marilyn and her husband Steve Patterson have two sons, John and Brent.

Weekly Reader Books presents

HELP IS ON
THE WAY
FOR:

Listening Skills

Written by Marilyn Berry
Pictures by Bartholomew

Living Skills Productions
Fallbrook, California

Weekly Reader Books offers several exciting
card and activity programs. For information,
write to WEEKLY READER BOOKS, P.O. Box 16636,
Columbus, Ohio 43216.

Executive Producer: Marilyn Berry
Editor: Theresa Tinkle
Consultants: Terie Snyder and Eleanor Villalpando
Design and Art Direction: Abigail Johnston
Typesetting: Curt Chelin

For a complete catalog of other living skills materials,
write to: Institute of Living Skills
P.O. Box 1461, Fallbrook, CA 92028

Weekly Reader Books edition published by
arrangement with Living Skills Press.

So you need to learn some **listening skills!**

Hang on! Help is on the way!

If you are having a hard time
- hearing what people say,
- understanding what people say,
- responding to what people say, or
- remembering what people say...

...you are not alone!

Just in case you're wondering...

...why don't we start at the beginning?

What Does It Mean To Listen?

To listen means to pay attention in order to hear. There are two types of listening: *passive* listening and *active* listening.

Passive listening is a relaxed activity that requires little effort or thought. An example of passive listening is listening to background music.

Active listening is an activity that requires more effort and thought. An example of active listening is listening to someone speak. When you listen to someone speak, you usually try to *hear* and *understand* what the person is saying.

Why Are Listening Skills Important?

Listening skills are tools that can help you to hear and understand what a person is saying. Good listening skills will help you
- hear more accurately,
- understand more of what you hear,
- respond appropriately to what you hear, and
- remember more of what you hear.

Listening is an important part of communication. The better your listening skills, the better you will communicate. Listening is also an important part of learning. The better your listening skills, the more you will learn. Listening skills can be easy to learn if you take it one step at a time.

Steps To Successful Listening

There are five simple steps you can follow that will help you become a successful listener:

- Eliminate the obstacles.
- Listen with your ears.
- Listen with your eyes.
- Listen with your mind.
- Respond to the message.

Step One: Eliminate The Obstacles

The first step to successful listening is to get rid of any obstacles that could keep you from hearing what the speaker is saying. Here are some common obstacles to look for:

Poor Reception
If you can't hear clearly, you can't listen. Make sure you are close enough to the speaker and that the speaker talks loudly and clearly enough for you to hear what is being said.

Outside Distractions

It is hard to listen to someone when there are things around you that take your attention away from the speaker. So that you can give the speaker your full attention, you may need to
- find a place without distractions,
- eliminate the distractions, or
- learn to ignore the distractions and focus on what is being said.

Inside Distractions

It is also hard to listen to someone when you have other thoughts on your mind. To give the speaker your full attention, you may need to

- put the other thoughts out of your mind and try to focus on what the speaker is saying, or
- suggest that the conversation take place at another time.

Step Two: Listen With Your Ears

The second step to successful listening is to listen carefully to *what* the speaker is saying and *how* he or she is saying it. You will need to listen carefully to the speaker's
- words and
- tone of voice.

The Speaker's Words

When someone is talking to you, it is important to listen carefully to his or her choice of words. You need to
- make sure you have heard the words correctly and
- listen to the words in the context of the message. Words can take on different meanings depending on how the speaker uses them.

The Speaker's Tone of Voice

When a person is talking to you, it is also important to notice his or her tone of voice. *How* a speaker says something can change the meaning of what he or she is saying. A person's tone of voice can tell you
- how the person feels about the subject and
- whether the person is serious or joking.

Step Three: Listening With Your Eyes

The third step to successful listening is to use your eyes to help you listen. When a person talks to you, he or she will most often use more than just words to communicate. Many times a person will use
- body language and
- visual aids

to get a point across.

Body Language

You will understand more of what a speaker is saying if you watch what the person is doing as he or she talks. You will want to watch the person's
- facial expressions,
- posture, and
- gestures.

Visual Aids

Many times a speaker will use a visual aid to help make a point. You will understand more of what the speaker is saying if you will look closely at the visual aid as you listen to the person talk.

Step Four: Listen With Your Mind

The fourth step to successful listening is to use your mind to help you understand and evaluate what the speaker is saying. When a person talks to you, you need to
- clarify the message,
- interpret the message, and
- examine the message.

Clarify the Message

To clarify means to make clear. When you clarify what someone is saying, you make sure that you are hearing the speaker correctly. You can clarify the message by
- asking questions about the message and
- putting the message in your own words.

Interpret the Message

One meaning of the word *interpret* is *explain*. Once you are sure you have heard the message correctly, you may still need some further explanation. To make sure you completely understand, you may need to ask the speaker to interpret the message for you.

Examine the Message

Once you understand what the speaker is saying, you need to take a closer look at the message. You need to think about

- how you feel about the message,
- whether you agree or disagree with the message, and
- what further information you need or want to know about the message.

Step Five: Respond To The Message

The final step to successful listening is to choose an appropriate response. The speaker needs to know that you have been listening and that you understand what he or she has been saying. Appropriate responses might be
- facial expressions,
- gestures,
- single words,
- simple statements,
- questions,
- long detailed comments.

Learning to use the five steps for successful listening is not hard. However, it does take some concentration and practice. The more you practice these steps, the more automatic they will become for you. Soon you will be using these listening skills without even thinking about them.

Tips For Successful Listening In School

You are required to spend a large part of every school day listening to your teachers. The five steps to successful listening will make listening in school much easier. There are also several tips that can help you improve your listening in school:

- Come to school prepared.
- Always be ready to listen.
- Know what to listen for.
- Remember what you hear.

Come To School Prepared

Listening in school is more meaningful and takes less effort when you come to school prepared to listen. Here are three things you can do to help prepare yourself:

1. **Keep up with your homework.** Many times the topics your teacher discusses on one day are related to the topics discussed the day before. Keeping up with your homework will give you some background for the new information that is being presented.

2. **Get some background information**. The more you know about a topic, the easier it is to listen to someone talk about it. If possible, try to get some background information on a topic *before* your teacher talks about it in class. Find out which topic your teacher plans to discuss the following day. Then either read a chapter ahead in your textbook or look up the topic in an encyclopedia.

3. **Make up a list of questions.** It is usually more interesting to listen to someone talk about a topic when you are curious about it. When you find out the topic your teacher will be discussing, write down a few questions that come to mind. As your teacher talks, try to listen for the answers.

Be Ready To Listen

An important tip for listening in school is to try always to be alert and ready to listen. You can make sure you are ready if you follow four simple rules:

1. **Choose a good seat.** Try to sit in a place where you can clearly see and hear the teacher. Remember also to choose a spot that is free from distractions.

2. **Don't talk or pass notes.** When you take time out from your listening to talk to a friend or write a friend a note, you could be missing some important information. Save your talking and note-passing for recess and lunch breaks. During class time try to keep your eyes and ears tuned in to the teacher.

3. **Don't doodle or daydream.** Doodling and daydreaming are both fun activities. However, when you do them in class, your attention is not where it needs to be. While you are in class, give the teacher and your schoolwork your full attention. Then set aside some time after school to doodle and daydream.

4. **Don't make up homework in class.** When you get behind in a subject, don't make up the work in another class. You will only fall further behind. If you listen carefully and pay attention during each class, you will have a better chance of keeping up with your work.

Know What To Listen For

Before your teacher shares information with the class, he or she has spent time making an outline of what to say. Sometimes your teacher will share the outline with the class so you can follow along. Your teacher might put the outline on the chalkboard or on a study sheet. This outline will give you a clue of what to listen for.

At other times you will be expected to find the outline on your own. As your teacher explains the topic to the class, you will be looking for two types of information:

1. The main ideas.
2. The supporting details.
This information is not hard to recognize when you know what to listen for.

The Main Ideas

When your teacher presents new information to your class, one of your goals is to pick out the most important points. The most important points are the *main ideas* of the talk. Most often these points are plainly stated in the introduction or summary of the talk. However, sometimes they are only suggested. You can find a main idea by asking yourself:

If you listen carefully, the teacher will sometimes give you clues that will help you find the main ideas. Listen for phrases such as these:

- "My first point is..."
- "This is important..."
- "You should know..."
- "Be sure to remember..."
- "Next, we'll talk about..."

Main ideas are sometimes repeated throughout the talk.

The Supporting Details

Supporting details are pieces of information that further explain the main ideas. Supporting details may include

- examples and stories,
- descriptions,
- definitions,
- facts,
- quotations, or
- questions.

If you listen carefully, the teacher will sometimes give you clues that will help you find the supporting details. Listen for key phrases such as these:

- "For example..."
- "The reasons for..."
- "The causes of..."
- "That reminds me of a story..."

Remember What You Hear

Information you hear in school is usually information you will need to remember. Here are three things that can help you remember what you hear in class:

1. Repeat the information.
2. Write down the information.
3. Use a tape recorder.

Repeat the Information

It is easier to remember important information if you hear it more than once. You can accomplish this by repeating the information to yourself.

- As soon as your teacher makes an important point, repeat the point in your mind.
- Sometime later that day, try to remember the important points and repeat them aloud.

Write Down the Information

It is also easier to remember important information that you hear if you write it down. As your teacher talks, write down the main ideas and their supporting details. Then read through your notes at a later time.

Use a Tape Recorder

A tape recorder can be a valuable listening aid. You may use it in class and record your teacher's talks. Later you will have more time to go over the talks and find the main ideas and supporting details. You may also read your notes into a recorder and listen to them over and over.

Some Final Notes

If you have a hard time listening in school, try setting up a reward system for yourself. It will be easier to listen in school if you have something to look forward to.

If you have trouble listening, you may have problems with your hearing. Ask your school nurse to check your hearing if you have any of these symptoms:

• There is a ringing in your ears.
• You often ask people to repeat what they say.
• You often misunderstand what people say.
• Things sound muffled.

WARNING!

If you follow the suggestions in this book, you will probably become a better listener and...

...you may also become a better student!

THE END

About the Author
Marilyn Berry has a master's degree in education with a specialization in reading. She is on staff as a creator of supplementary materials at Living Skills Press. Marilyn and her husband Steve Patterson have two sons, John and Brent.